HOW TO MINE CRYPTOCURRENCIES STEP BY STEP

Content

The basics to get started in cryptocurrency mining 4
How to mine 7
Basic mining considerations 8
Aspects of cryptocurrency mining profitability 9
Profitability calculators you can use 13
The algorithms used by mining 16
The requirements to carry out cryptocurrency mining 18
Interest earned on cryptocurrencies 23
Requirements for mining cryptocurrencies using PoS 25
How to choose the right cryptocurrency to mine 26
All about a mining pool 28
The form of payment of the pools 30
The role of web miners 31
What mining in the cloud represents 33
Mining cryptocurrencies on a Mac 34
Ethereum mining via Ubuntu Linux 35
How to mine Litecoin 41
Learn how to mine Monero using your computer 47
Find out how to mine Zcash 56
Mining vs. investment; considerations when starting out 61
Minimum hardwares to mine Zcash and Ethereum 67
The best GPU for Ethereum mining 72
Current Bitcoin mining facilities 75
The best software to practice Ethereum mining 77

A mining requires power and at the same time a good level of performance, that way the process can be realized, so it is a synonym that investment is required, to obtain ASIC equipment; Application Specific Circuit, which are specially created to carry out mining with striking power.

Mining can be done jointly through a pool or cooperative, where the majority of the members work together to receive rewards, because a higher level of power is pooled, and in turn they can solve a block to achieve the goal set, this is not another type of mining but a grouping.

Computers that work together to obtain rewards can divide the profits obtained through different modes, but it is not a mandatory mode for mining, far from it.

Basic mining considerations

Starting to carry out mining is not a simple step, but a whole procedure must be carried out beforehand, so that it is possible to assemble a feasible equipment, which goes beyond the simple choice of the computer, but depends on the type of equipment and the cost of obtaining it.

Similarly, another factor that is vital to take into account is the competition that may be present during that moment in which

sion, but in the market also looks the option of Dogecoin, BitTorrent, HUSD, Stellar, TRON, Polkadot, Cardano, NEO, Dai, IOTA, and many more.

- **Minar**

The action of mining is based on creating cryptocurrencies as they are earned or obtained, this type of reward is presented during a successful process, but generates that it is not necessary to buy the cryptocurrencies, but to obtain as many rewards as possible.

How to mine

In order to undertake cryptocurrency mining, it is required to implement the resolution of mathematical calculations by means of the help of computing power, i.e. the user lends the equipment to the operation of P2P networks to fulfill the calculations that arise, thereby processing transactions.

That is to say that the transaction is carried out with mathematical calculations performed by means of computers that are kept running 24 hours a day, every day to produce a constant consumption, so it is not an activity that you can perform by means of a basic or domestic computer.

This control or power of these assets, not only resides on the P2P users, but the mining contributes to the creation of cryptocurrencies, this type of dynamics changes according to the type of cryptocurrencies, and as one participates in this process, the rewards for the miners originate, which means receiving units of these virtual currencies.

- **Reliability and legality**

Definitely cryptocurrency mining is legal and imposes security, but some provisions must be applied so that problems do not arise, one of the most mandatory measures is to take care of the creation of a private key so that your funds are not at risk, in case of using it, care must be taken.

Added to this is the diversity of existing cryptocurrencies, because the number is growing every day and the profitability varies for each one, this must be taken into account during the profitability estimation but also when deciding on one asset and another, the most popular are Litecoin, Ether, Dash, Ripple, Monero others that may be to your liking.

Similarly, the type of hardware you select to mine has an important weight, so it is a set of factors involved in each deci-

tools that help to know if it is a profitable measure, these calculations can be performed on a custom basis, but can not be taken as a 100% effective result.

However, by means of cryptocurrency calculators, they work as an aid to be clear about some criteria but to get to that point, the first thing is to know all the basic aspects with which you have contact during mining, where the following aspects stand out:

- **Cryptocurrencies**

The main asset generated by mining is cryptocurrencies, which are virtual currencies that have become a favorite means of virtual payment, thanks to the fact that they are digital assets that are not tangible, because they are mobilized by means of encrypted transfers that can be extended to merchants or businesses.

A quality of these assets is that it is called a self-regulated unit, because there is no institution that intervenes on its control, causing its value not to be modified, but to change based on the movements of the users themselves as they carry out Peer to Peer exchanges.

Frequently cryptocurrency mining became a popular topic nowadays, but at the same time there are doubts about its profitability and legality, but to reach those answers it must be determined that it means an activity that contributes a series of processes that help to validate transactions coming from a cryptocurrency.

Specifically, the miner's function is focused on solving puzzles, for which special equipment is implemented that requires certain consumption considerations, such as internet and electricity, depending on the cryptocurrency because not all of them work in the same way.

The basics to get started in cryptocurrency mining

Cryptocurrency mining is an activity that you need to consider very wisely, especially because with information it is easier to dare, also taking into account whether it is a profitable activity or not in your situation, because this measure depends on different factors.

The calculation of profitability of cryptocurrency mining, involves analysis of how you plan to operate, but you can use

you get ready to mine, without forgetting the expense that represents the power consumption because they are devices that will be connected for 24 hours, so they will require cooling to avoid overloading devices.

As these factors have an influence on mining, the profitability of the cryptocurrency at that moment cannot be left aside, for this reason cryptocurrency mining changes according to the type of asset you have selected to start this activity.

Aspects of cryptocurrency mining profitability

The profitability of cryptocurrency mining is complex to determine or establish, because it always varies in each case or situation, especially in the moment in which the income on that cryptocurrency is produced, in addition to the value of the electricity and the mining hardware according to the country in which the investment is made.

All these variables are crucial to establish profitability, but to this is added the amount you are willing to invest, all this can be simplified in the use of specific calculators that summarize this task, so that by filling in some data of these variables you can approximate a number a little more accurate.

A more realistic vision about this activity is what will allow it to be evaluated to recognize if it is worth it or not, especially for what must be invested such as electricity, refrigeration, equipment and also the password, this in turn is solved by determining the type of cryptocurrency you want to mine.

You will not always get the same profitability from one cryptocurrency or another, much less at different times, because everything changes every day, so all these details are needed to make an accurate calculation, you can enter this on a tool that studies this type of information so you can decide.

To use these online calculators you only have to add reliable data, to recognize the profitability of these steps or activity, also if in your country or environment the cost of energy is negligible you can get more profit when performing this type of activity, the aspects that influence are as follows:

1. **Hash rate**

It is one of the most important measures, because it is the unit to measure the power in which cryptocurrencies are processed, it is located within one of the basic aspects to recognize the amount of computational operations that can be performed from the computer, to know this you can investigate online the model of your computer.

2. Amount of electricity consumption

The amount of electricity is known as what the equipment you use for mining demands, this from the first instance demands that it is an activity that can not be carried out from a laptop or tablet, but it is computers that meet an optimum power level.

On the other hand, care must be taken that the mining equipment does not overheat, so it is vital to think about the inclusion of an air conditioner on the site so that the state of the room is not hot and harmful to the equipment.

3. Cost of electricity

Based on the tariff of the contracted electricity services of the place where you are going to mine, you can make a calculation on the consumption, and even consider whether it would be appropriate to make a change of place, because mining represents a constant operation, this represents a constant payment that is subject to price changes and the profitability of the cryptocurrency.

4. **Hardware cost**

Hardware, once purchased, represents a one-time cost, but it cannot be overlooked that in the course of mining you may need to buy better equipment, or you may have purchased regular equipment and then the demands of mining itself pushes you to upgrade the level of equipment.

5. **Pool rate**

Being in a pool is a choice that may be convenient for many, but requires the coverage of an entry fee or the percentage you must pay, this type of data is often omitted.

6. **Software commission**

The cost that is part of the software commission is composed by a measure to be taken into account, so that the comparative or calculators can yield a profitability index.

As you can enter this data on the calculator, the value of the cryptocurrency is closely followed, in addition to the level of difficulty behind the cryptocurrency, to keep this in mind when thinking about rewards, these values likewise possess other options to make it a profitable activity.

The biggest advantage of mining is concentrated on the type of cryptocurrency you choose to mine, that is why the value of these assets must be measured in real time, to follow the price and the type of fluctuations that exist behind the virtual currency, this is assumed by the digital calculators to make the best decision.

Profitability calculators you can use

The number of calculators for measuring profitability varies completely, but the functions are generic for most of them, the important thing is to define the data that the boxes ask for so that the results can help you to have a clear view, but some may omit the calculation of the value of the software or other similar value.

But the operation of this kind of calculators is similar, so you can use the one you find easier to use, they are still the best way to follow closely the profitability in real time, to opt for the cryptocurrency that is providing better bonuses, and consider the one that is more complicated to mine.

The most commonly used tools for measuring mining profitability are as follows:

- **CoinWarz**

It is postulated as one of the simplest tools, because you can choose the type of algorithm you want, and then fill in the sections that appear on the calculator, in addition to this calculation is also responsible for showing the best cryptocurrencies to follow that mobility of profitability today.

In the selection of coins you can press to get a whole graph, on which you can add data that shows the level of profitability and the benefits generated by cryptocurrencies from their advantages, rewards and above all costs, all of which can be measured in a simple way.

The cryptocurrency query is available, to have access to data such as Litecoin, Ethereum, Dash, Zcash, Monero, and others that are in the section of this tool, as the qualities of these virtual currencies are followed.

- **CryptoCompare**

It has been classified as one of the best cryptocurrency profitability calculators, as it allows the study of a wide variety of virtual currencies, from its platform you can get details about these assets, from their price to relevant news such as tips.

On the other hand, a relevant quality of this calculator is that all the data are issued in a simple way, so the order helps to be understood without so much complication, from the "Markets" section you can find "Mining calculator", from that section data of the hashing power level are integrated.

Measuring the energy consumed is a reality by this tool, the same happens to estimate the percentage of Pool, so that the result can be really attached to the way you are going to mine, and then change and know the value of each cryptocurrency that is of your preference.

- **Whattomine**

It represents a good web alternative to follow the profitability of cryptocurrencies, thanks to its complete operation and offers a great variety of information, where each data can be filtered and ordered according to your preference, then to obtain the final calculation you only have to select the currency you want.

On a section of the platform you will find information to complete such as values, data, hash rate, energy, cost and other percentages, so you can also take into consideration to visualize the difficulty of mining, even consult any variety of cryptocurrencies.

- **CoinCalculators**

It has the same functions as the previous calculators, but with a more practical interface to handle it as you wish, because from the "coins" section you can come across revelations about the best hardwares to carry out mining for example, so you can take the step towards mining with greater security.

By filling in all the data, such as hashrate, cost of energy or hardware and others, you can check the level of profitability offered by this activity, without losing sight of the distinction between one asset or another to recognize its profitability.

The algorithms used by mining

Carrying out Bitcoin mining, consists in the participation on the verification of transactions that are carried out over the network, to issue new cryptocurrencies, in case you are interested by this type of mining, you should closely follow all the requirements of the algorithm domain of this activity, because two types of algorithms are used for mining, such as the following:

1. Mining algorithm

It is recognized as a data processing, for this you need specialized hardware that works with this type of algorithm, depending on which you use will require the implementation of equipment that have the ability to deal with these qualities, in the case of ASIC devices, are responsible for working for specific algorithms.

2. Consensus algorithm

It is an algorithm related to all members or nodes that are part of a cryptocurrency network, following the operation of the same, because some transactions fulfill a particular purpose or validity, all this influences the block order that is implemented on the chain, and other aspects.

The most popular consensus algorithms are the proof of work (PoW) and the proof of participation (PoS), additionally there are doubts about the amount of work that is required on the proof of work, to which you should keep in mind that it is a lower level of work, because it is not an obligation that you must do on your own, but the hardware takes care of it.

The proof of work is described as a consensus algorithm to solve a puzzle, within this dynamic the miner seeks to find the answer as soon as possible so that it can integrate a new block that belongs to the chain transactions, this works because it is very unlikely that two miners can come up with the same solution.

Each riddle used for the blocks needs different solutions in a random order, this type of mechanism causes that it is not possible to search for double coins, so for each solution a reward is generated and to find the answer it is necessary to apply the mining hardwares to process data at high speed.

This is the reason why miners must have powerful equipment, that way the cryptocurrency you selected can be mined, in this sense the proof of work is one of the most used consensus algorithms, especially when it comes to Bitcoin, being one of the first virtual currencies and employs PoW.

This kind of mining requires special hardware, this is the same in the case of selecting Monero, Zcash, Ethereum classic, Bitcoin cash, and others, but the Ethereum network possesses a substitution by proof-of-stake or is maintained by a hybrid function.

Requirements for mining cryptocurrencies

A key to be part of cryptocurrency mining is to sustain a continuous learning, to advance in this activity and to obtain profits with a high dose of patience, especially to have the necessary hardware and software to make it a profitable action, and without overlooking the costs that this action causes.

But above obtaining these devices, you must implement a cooling system so that the location does not suffer from overheating failures, the most important thing is that both electricity and internet can be stable, otherwise the work will be interrupted and you can not exercise mining, promptly what you need is as follows:

- **Hardware**

The hardware issue refers directly to the key equipment to mine the selected cryptocurrency, this includes in general line everything related to processors, graphic cards and other special equipment, once you can select one, you can advance to fit other qualities.

But what can be taken into account is the type of mining algorithm, on which the cryptocurrency you are going to mine is associated or programmed, because the mining algorithm is the main responsible for compliance with the rules at the time of encrypting or decrypting the information that arises after each transaction.

That is to say, by means of the algorithm a simple message is obtained for understanding until it becomes undecipherable, in addition this is the way so that the result cannot be repeated, as part of the security of the network, that is to say, it is the way through which the cryptocurrency cannot be counterfeited.

For this reason, if you want to mine Bitcoin, you must implement ASIC devices, as it is the best solution to be applied on the SHA-256 algorithm, but to mine Ethereum or also Zcash, it demands a dedicated graphics card (GPU), in addition to using a power supply that is 100% certified.

On the other hand, to mine Monero or bytecoin, it is necessary to meet a requirement of a computer CPU processor, to fulfill mining effectively and reap profits.

- **Software**

There are different types of software or programs designed to mine cryptocurrencies, even of the size of Bitcoin, so the first thing is to have mining software, where the hardware will be able to start up the hardware, to develop a performance on the network of the cryptocurrency so that it can be mined.

For this reason you can currently find different types of software, it all depends on the type of hardware you are using, as well as considering the type of cryptocurrency you want to mine, the most used are CGminer and Claymore, the first is the most used to mine Bitcoin cash, while the second is ideal for ether.

In the same way, you must incorporate a program to measure the performance of the hardware, and you can configure the performance of these utilities to follow your preferences, in the case of the use of ASIC devices, such as Bitmain's Ant-Miner, it offers an autonomous system for configuration and monitoring.

But if you are mining through GPU, it is necessary to download and use programs such as MSI Afterburner or GPU-Z to fulfill the purpose of mining, concerning the mining rig known as performance, can be obtained from the website of the mining pool or appealing to the functions of TeamViewer as it offers access to the rig remotely.

- **Wallet or purse**

An indispensable requirement is to have a wallet, to store the payments you receive when mining, this can be of different modalities such as hardware, a cold wallet, or software that works as an application, in the case of cold wallets it is more reliable equipment, although the software can be protected with strong passwords.

Online you must beware of hacks, the same happens with some exchange houses, so it is better to opt for the first options to put your assets at risk for any reason.

- **Refrigeration and air conditioning**

A key requirement that cannot be overlooked is the conditioning of the area, because the mining equipment must be in accordance or under a stable temperature so that its operation is not affected, especially when the level of processing to which they are subjected generates extreme heat that can cause deterioration.

So that the equipment cannot overheat, the care of the temperature is everything, because that helps the devices can provide an extensive duration without stopping working, although all this must be submitted under constant evaluation, a key data is to investigate the maximum temperature that supports the hardware you use.

The temperature must be guarded, so that you have peaks of what is capable of reaching a device during mining, this also helps to get a less harmful point to exercise mining, a control of this level is beneficial for the equipment to be safe, this can be exercised by closely following some points that prevent overheating.

The first key or answer is refrigeration, because it is what must be preserved in a space, the solution lies on the air conditioners and constant ventilation, likewise on the equipment can be applied liquid cooling systems, to be used as a form of maintenance.

On top of the cooling, there is the configuration at the time of mining, this means that the assigned power can be controlled over the heat extractors that are part of the hardware, this goes hand in hand with the processing power that can be designated.

The most usual is that the mining power is lowered a little, so that the equipment can work better for a long time, because if you have devices at the maximum level, some failures may occur much earlier than expected based on the qualities of the equipment, which affects the level of income you spend on mining.

Interest accrued by cryptocurrencies

Many cryptocurrencies selected for mining have an interest-based protocol and operation, because the system rewards each participant for collecting cryptocurrencies over a specific network, thereby validating each transaction, known as proof of participation.

The proof-of-stake protocol does not maintain a high energy consumption when validating transactions, or to issue cryptocurrencies, this is a big difference it has with the proof-of-work, that is why the proof-of-stake consists of the amount of cryptocurrencies that have been accumulated.

To be part of the validation of a PoS network it is vital to have cryptocurrencies that will be used for this activity, then this type of cryptocurrency must be blocked on the blockchain, thus certifying that the funds are not used for any purpose other than validating transactions.

This means that you will be offering a guarantee on security, and on the behavior of the network itself, because if you exercise an inappropriate action you will have the cryptocurrencies blocked, within this dynamic the selection of the validator node is added to the next block in a random way.

But as you own more cryptocurrencies for this type of utility, you raise the possibility of being selected and you are going to get a higher profit margin, however the main reason why Peercoin, PIVX, NEO and Lisk are preferred for the less negative impact it causes to the environment.

Requirements for mining cryptocurrencies using PoS

The task of validating transactions by means of PoS does not require a high level of power consumption, so it is not necessary to have specialized hardware, you only need a computer with a hard drive capable of holding a copy of blockchain, without leaving aside the role of a good internet connection.

In the midst of this procedure you don't have to manage the whole node to get money, there are pools for cryptocurrencies that perform their functions in the same way as proof-of-work mining pools do, it is important on this dynamic that you can share the profits based on the participation.

On the other hand, there are requirements for each network, especially when you want to have the nodes validated, but these are security or scalability issues that are based on the expectations of cryptocurrencies, for this you can follow the mining calculators to follow the signs of the cryptoasset market.

How to choose the cryptocurrency to mine

A crucial point when getting involved in the world of cryptocurrencies is to follow the profitability of any form of monetization of the same, for this you must study some variables about these assets, one of these details is the current price that the cryptocurrency has in the market, as well as the cost of electricity.

Also the mining power is crucial when making a decision, because some cryptocurrencies demand much more power, the same happens with the purchase of hardware, this type of data can create a profile of the ideal cryptocurrency for mining, likewise websites such as WhatToMine or CoinWarz can help.

The evaluation to decide on one cryptocurrency and another, can also be measured by its performance, this view can provide more security when making a decision, but under a long-term scale, so it is a step that deserves a high level of seriousness, this is complicated when you have in mind some novel cryptocurrency.

But what should be evaluated the most are the security aspects, and exchange without problems, so it is a must to investigate the type of project that is behind a cryptocurrency, because that way you can take advantage of the growth, and knowing the use or role that the asset has is easier.

The evaluation of the type of hardware or software needed represents another measure to know if it is positive to mine them, without leaving aside the characteristics that are behind the virtual currency, this means that it must be investigated from the most general of the cryptocurrency to the most specific.

Through the white paper you can know about an asset, since you can find the explanation of the project, this offers data from the technical relevance but also on the ethical, this is compared with the roadmap of the project to measure the extent to which you want to reach that cryptocurrency and the time frame to achieve it.

The reality or opinion of other miners is a point to take into account, because in the middle of many forums or chats you can find a common decision, this type of aspects are the ones that allow you to better evaluate cryptocurrencies based on your expectations, where the role of the developers of the same also matter.

All about a mining pool

The mining pool works as a node, it allows a group of cryptocurrency miners to connect, so that the activity can be performed simultaneously, causing the mining power to grow significantly, this is part of the hashrate values, so that everyone participates in the network as a single connection.

This type of bets have been verified to work much better on the proof of work, because for the proof of participation it has a totally different use, where the theme is that the participants can designate decision making power to another to be able to manage the node.

This means that the possibility for more blocks to be integrated into the chain becomes effective and thus the rewards increase, in the case of PoW or PoS the receipt of rewards is always allocated according to the pool agreement so that they are effectively distributed.

The doubt between mining alone or accompanied, can be huge, but instinct matters as well as following the guidance of reality to not make a decision that exceeds your chances of responding with a team, because all this goes hand in hand with the type of profit you can get through mining.

But the crucial point is that if you want to mine cryptocurrencies on your own, you must have a previous investment to have the necessary equipment, but if you do it with a half investment, you will not reach the mining power required to reap profits.

When it comes to power, more output is generated by an entire network than by a single device, so performing the activity as a group is beneficial, and this causes them to create more equipment farms so that the mining of any one device is completely nullified.

As mining is based on finding a correct result on the cryptocurrency network, the possibility of resolution rises with a high mining power such as that achieved by a pool, because it is greater than any other node operating in the network, when mining alone, you gather 1% hashrate, instead per group increases up to 10% with 8 miners for example.

That is why in a group it is usually more profitable according to the effectiveness of the mining power they can gather, this is the main reason why it is chosen, pool mining is usually much more convenient especially in comparison of equipment, in the face of this may arise the doubt of opting for Monero which is an anti-ASIC cryptocurrency.

An option such as Monero is feasible because it is associated with CPU and GPU mining, but also if you have a lower mining level the smartest thing to do is to think and bet on a pool, you can check through CoinWarz the estimated time in which the first block will be mined and what will be obtained.

The values of the network are taken into account to think about the profitability of each adjustment or decision, but in addition to the time it takes to mine on your own, you must think that getting involved with a pool can generate a significant amount of royalties, the worst of either measure is that the price of the cryptocurrency declines.

The form of payment of the pools

The form of payment of the pools is associated with a form of distribution, which varies according to the company or the agreements, but most of them focus on an equitable distribution, based on the mining power of each participant, and the reward is developed by means of two parts or two processes.

One stage of collection through the pools is for the new cryptocurrencies that are issued along with the transaction fees, or the administrators keep the proceeds to distribute the new cryptocurrencies, depending on how the devices are used, the administrators can charge a percentage of what has been mined.

This type of fee or charge has to do with the maintenance of the pool, but beyond accepting and finding favorable payment conditions for your case, it is still advisable to measure the profitability, looking at the devices that reach the necessary and significant mining power to reach an optimal hashrate, but this is synonymous to an investment on the hardware.

The role of web miners

The definition of web miners focuses on a type of software that can be installed from a code base, this comes from the website that causes the computers of each visiting user and their device to be used for mining, the installation of this kind of software is done by the web administrator or by an attacker.

This kind of mining is distinguished as a malware, that is to say as a malicious software that is why it must issue a warning about its function because if you do not authorize this kind of step, it would be an illicit measure, even if it is not designed by the administrator himself, this causes web miners to be associated with superpowers.

In general this kind of mining is a responsibility, because this technology should be dedicated for a fair use, that way users are not affected in a negative way, since an inappropriate utility can be classified as one, because without consulting it affects the performance of the computers that enter the portal.

The deterioration of a device is due to the fact that cryptocurrency mining demands a higher level of CPU, in the event that the device does not have the necessary qualities to meet the demands of the CPU, as a result it begins to operate much slower, and in the case of phones it begins to suffer irreparable damage.

But over and above these evil functions, web miners in the right hands can have a much better application, as some charitable causes may opt for this alternative by prior authorization, as well as this or other projects allow you to choose how much processing you can donate so as not to overload your computer.

This means that web miners are employed as an additional option to set up paid subscriptions, or as a form of advertising on websites, this is acceptable as long as prior authorization is issued, this is associated with the mining power you are also willing to provide.

What cloud mining represents

This is a service where you can rent a mining power, that way you can get the rewards you have obtained, it is like a type of mining but done through third parties, thanks to the platform that provides a part of its mining power, this causes more doubts about the profitability compared to doing it alone.

Within cloud mining the same factors come together to study pool mining, therefore it can be understood as a type of relative profitability, but you must consider the risk of being scammed because through the cloud this is more frequent or under a much greater danger.

The positive thing about mining in the cloud is that you do not have to invest in the purchase of hardware, in addition to reducing the cost of electricity, cooling and other concepts of this type, the same applies to the maintenance or care of the hardware, because it will not be a matter of concern.

The only downside is the incidence of being scammed, because the mining power is not originated by yourself, for that reason you cannot notice the full mining power they offer and the agreement cancellation conditions are not favorable for you, and they can make them effective if the cryptocurrency market prices are not convenient.

Cryptocurrency mining from a Mac

Mac users may be hesitant to participate in cryptocurrency mining, especially since the community of OS users may have less opportunity to be part of this activity, but it should not be overlooked that the average user with Windows or Linux must also have computing power that their computers may not possess.

This is due to the evolution of this kind of technology, especially the manufacture of special hardware such as ASICs, or the same happens with GPU cards that have a powerful development, so mining with the use of personal computers has been left aside.

The world of mining is directly associated with high temperatures, power consumption and computers, all of this is a professional environment to make money through this field, but above all this scenario, it is possible to generate money using Mac, although it would not be the same magnitude that other equipment generates.

For all these reasons, it is not a good idea to mine from Mac, even Windows does not have wide acceptance, but it is best to invest for the higher computational capacity, to face the existing competition on this blockchain network that you want to mine.

The mission is to enter the world of mining through savings, to implement and use specialized software, along with knowledge to understand the operation of these devices.

Ethereum mining via Ubuntu Linux

Ethereum works as a network that has great similarity with Bitcoin, but its quality resides on the participation or use on smart contracts, this is an advance on the transaction environment as it promotes privacy and anonymity, this is the potential that resides under the Ethereum project.

From this reasoning increases the interest in mining Ethereum, but it is an action that is not as profitable as it is believed, however there is an opportunity to monetize through this means, to reach that result you must have graphics processing power, being the GPU the most key.

One of the best options for mining is the choice of NVIDIA GeForce GTX 1070, it is postulated as one of the best cards for this purpose, because above the processing power it provides, it also decreases the energy impact, this is essential for costs to drop a little and yield higher profits.

Having covered the issue of graphics cards, the next thing to address is the issue of software, because it is what allows you to be part of the network to distribute and mine, this is not advisable to do through Windows, as it is much more effective to opt for Linux.

A system such as Linux has more freedoms because the operating system is free, and reduces the expense of mining because the mining is effective up to a higher hash rate than would be obtained through Windows, implementing the same hardware, these are clear differences between one and the other.

For project servers, the use of Linux is the most indicated, the evolution of the same one causes that it is a more frequent download than it is believed, to carry out the process of use of the software you must install Ubuntu, when you have the Linux equipment the rest will be to execute and to configure the program.

- **Ubuntu installation requirements**

To use Ubuntu you need to have a USB stick that is at least 2GB, then you need to download Etcher which is available for operating systems such as Windows, Mac and Linux, finally you can install Ubuntu, after formatting the USB stick and start Etcher to follow the steps of the installer.

- **Ubuntu Installation**

The installer process itself requests access to the Ubuntu location, after this step you can connect the USB memory on the machine so that the system boots from it, this is guided by the installer that works intuitively, you only have to select the operating system on which it will be installed.

Normally it is better not to partition the disk, but to leave Ubuntu in full operation, also you can extend the disk capacity by investing in a SSD worthwhile, after completing these installation options you can disconnect the USB stick to reboot the machine and enter directly on Ubuntu.

- **Enter the software to mine Ethereum**

To mine Ethereum you must start Geth and Ethminer, install the correct drivers for the graphics cards, and finally use or have a wallet to receive the funds that you are mining, when fulfilling this you only have to follow the steps from a terminal window.

The complete operation of the Ubuntu launcher is located on the upper left corner of the interface you are using, and it can be activated by means of a shortcut with the Windows key, so you can type terminal and the button to run the application appears.

Then the first thing to do is to install the APT repository that is part of Ethereum, by entering the command:

Sudo apt - get install

Software-properties-common

Sudo add-apt-repository

Ppa: ethereum/ethereum

Sudo apt - get update

You can then proceed to install geth and ethminer by entering the following commands:

Sudo apt - get install

Ethereum ethmier geth

Covered these steps, the next thing to do is to make sure you have the card drivers installed, that way you will have the support to perform Ethereum mining, if you don't cover this step, you will have to deal with open source Linux drivers that don't help much.

If you are going to install the drivers you must take into account that the installation cannot be carried out if Ubuntu is running, to exit you can use the commands Crtl + Alt + F1, then it will be necessary to enter the user and password, to stop the X server, you can press the following:

Sudo service lightdm stop

In this way you can run the graphics card driver with total freedom, you can not overlook to switch to the folder where the download was made, once you comply with this installation what is needed is to restart the computer, by means of the command:

Ethminer -list-devices

The exposed list must be equal to the same number of cards that you own or have installed, in addition to the total name and memory must be correct, if there is any error it means that the driver is not working properly and there was an error during the previous process, in case of being correct, the next thing to apply is:

Ethminer -M -G

In the case of the -M it refers to Ethminer, while the -G is what is going to be executed with the GPUs that have been installed, this kind of command when started for the first time starts a DAG, this takes between 8 and 15 minutes, then you will be able to visualize the minimum hash rate, the maximum and the average.

To finish applying the configuration it is vital to add the wallet to receive the Ethereum that are mined, or any you wish to receive, this merits the installation of geth that allows you to create the wallet so that you only have to create a good password that offers guarantees, through the command entered:

Geth account new

Controlling this key is crucial so that no one can take action with your Ethereum funds, you can't forget it either because there is no way to rocover the password, these precautions represent the success of the mining operation.

- **Select a pool**

When you have the software ready to mine, the next thing to do is to be part of a pool, because it is better to bet on a much more collective mining power to get a block than to work on your own and have less chances to achieve it, but beforehand you should know that the profits are shared according to your contribution or your activity.

To implement an effective Ethereum mining it is vital or more advisable to be part of a pool, to make the right decision you can follow the Ethereum forums and recognize a pool that fits your needs, when selecting it you must have the address that is included on ethminer, in addition to completing other fields such as your wallet.

Ethminer -U -F "http://eth-eu.dwarfpool.com:80/wallet

Through the pool's website you can find each of these data, such as the address, port, and other details that are key to start mining, most of the pools are kept anonymous and you do not have to register to be part of it, likewise the effectiveness of the pool can be measured by its statistics.

How to mine Litecoin

If you are thinking of mining Litecoin there are many points to consider and know, the first thing to discover is that it is a network that takes 2.5 minutes to confirm each block, so it represents one of the assets that works four times faster, this is an interesting point to consider this asset to mine it.

The popularity of an asset such as Litecoin makes it an attractive option for mining, especially because it can be carried out through a wide variety of options, and each one is suitable for different budgets, you can evaluate the following modalities:

1. **Solo mining**

This is known as assuming the responsibility of investing and obtaining all the necessary equipment to develop mining, but this has the advantage of not having to divide or share profits, so you can get more money by being exempt from commission, but the investment is made at the beginning to have the equipment.

The same happens with the payment of the services, since they must be assumed individually, therefore it is a measure that for many can be costly and not be the indicated option they expect so much, in addition to this, if you do not develop a good mining power you can spend an important lapse of time without obtaining profits.

2. Mining well

In case solo mining looks expensive, you can study the role of the mining pit, because it is a modality where resources are shared, be it computational power or electricity, which at the same time increases the opportunity to get the reward behind the block.

By means of this alternative the income is more constant, because when mining in each opportunity the percentage is distributed according to what you provide in terms of energy or power, that is why currently there are a lot of options of mining shafts such as the following:

- **Litecoin Mining Pool.** It is recognized as one of the oldest pools because it operates since 2011, it also maintains a policy in which it does not charge commission, this works by a pay per share (PPS) system, which indicates that the reward is distributed according to the energy and electricity provided.
- **Antpool.** It is located in China and is recognized as one of the largest wells, it does not charge commission when joining but they keep a percentage of the

transactions with the rewards, these are divided according to the shared energy that is able to release payments daily.

These are the pioneers, but you can find many more online, the important thing is that you can consult through a forum, that way you can measure the dynamics they use and if it is profitable for you.

3. **Mining in the cloud**

In order not to have to contribute anything at the time of mining, that is, not to have to buy expensive equipment, the opportunity or last option is to opt for mining in the cloud, because you only have to pay a platform so that this alternative takes care of working for you, so the only requirement is to have a computer.

This kind of platform works as a group of computers that have a setting to perform cryptocurrency mining, as you have more computers interconnected, it means you can mine effectively, this in turn is a great start for beginners, because you don't have to invest in expensive hardware.

But care should be dedicated on the type of mining company you select, because online abound a lot of scammers who take your money, so long before betting on any should be investigated previously, one of the best known and safe is Hashflare, for its track record since 2014.

- **Litecoin mining hardware**

At first Litecoin mining could be carried out only with the CPU and GPU, which involves a small investment to start with, and you can still find significant profits, but then this has moved towards potentially finding higher profits, using ASICs equipment to mine.

The performance of ASICs is greater than a CPU or GPU, so it implies a substantial increase in profits, because it is a better equipment to reach those profitable results that everyone expects, for this reason very little CPU and GPU is used, because they are obsolete, this causes that the necessary elements for this mining are the following:

1. **Antminer L3+.** It is one of the most powerful hardwares for Litecoin mining, it is the most powerful and endorsed by BitMain, so the other hardware does not have this level of popularity, yielding a hash rate of 504MH/s to solve mathematical equations effectively.

In the market you can continue to investigate a second option that can generate a good hash rate, so you can get good results when mining.

- **Litecoin mining software**

The key piece for which software is sought is for the Antminer L3+, which for its ease of adjustment makes it ideal to combine with software of the size of a mining pit, to get the right one you can investigate, and then from the BitMain site you can create an account, then configure it and add the URL of the mining group.

Option	Description
Pool URL	Enter the URL of your desired pool.
	The AntMiner L3+ can be set up with three mining pools, with decreasing priority from the first pool (pool 1) to the third pool (pool 3). The pools with low priority will only be used if all higher priority pools are offline.
Worker	Your worker ID on the selected pool.
Password	The password for your selected worker.

- **The Litecoin price**

It is essential to take into account the value and the type of fluctuation that Litecoin can experience, because it is a volatile asset, you should also consider other ways of mining that can be useful for you, such as entering the world of this asset through the purchase in an Exchange for trading.

Learn how to mine Monero using your computer

The mining that is part of Monero is special, because it is one of the few that can be performed from the use of the CPU, so it is one of the simplest alternatives to carry out mining, even for beginners it is a great way to adapt to that dynamic, and it is positive because it is one of the best quoted assets today.

Before making any decision when mining cryptocurrencies, you should understand the kind of conditions required to make a profit, one of the most fundamental requirements is the technical knowledge of the whole procedure, as well as equipping the area with a good power supply to make it stable, but at the same time economical.

The mining process requires a significant level of capital, and a high dose of patience to wait for the achievement of profits, without overlooking the verification of the legal situation of mining in the country, and not to neglect the maintenance of the equipment as you can generate profits.

Similarly, the installation of mining software requires GNU/Linux, since it is open source and there is less chance of encountering a virus problem or suffering constant vulnerabilities, but it is more common to use Windows for this type of activity.

- ## The RandomX algorithm

The development of Monero mining is focused on the RandomX algorithm, because it has a striking performance on CPUs, for this reason it is not necessary to implement ASICs, motivating more people to get involved in the mining activity.

RandomX is described as an algorithm that offers randomized operation, thus the processes indispensable for mining, so ASIC devices are not effective in decentralizing the ecosystem, which means that you need only a computer that is suitable for mining activity.

- ## Requirements to mine Monero

The equipment to perform Monero mining is a PC, laptop, notebook or any device of professional character that is capable of working 24 hours a day, 7 days a week, this means that the more technical qualities they have, the better performance they offer on mining.

What is recommended is to use a computer or CPU, which is a 64-bit operating system, either Windows or GNU/Linux, 4-thread or CPU core with at least 4GB of RAM, with a stable broadband internet connection, likewise this equipment should be prepared with special software for Monero and its mining.

Usually the software used is from XMR-Rig because of its simplicity, additionally it is vital to have a wallet compatible with Monero, in order to have a place to receive the profits generated by the mining shares.

- **Steps and procedure for mining in Monero**

The mining process that Monero requires, can be easily understood by following certain steps, once you are able to complete them you can get to practice mining until you make a profit:

1. Create the Monero wallet (XMR)

A first basic action is to create a Monero Wallet (XMR), since it works to obtain deposits that are generated by the mining activity, it is best to use the ones that come from the official website of Monero, in the "Downloads" section and then click on the "GUI Wallet" option.

When you go to the Wallet option, you can download the Windows version that works only for 64-bit systems. Before downloading, you can check that it is a genuine version so that you do not install a virus or a suspicious code is leaked.

2. **Log in and launch the Wallet**

Once you have downloaded the wallet and installed it, you can run it to configure the language theme, and the mode of the wallet execution, in that sense the simple mode means that the wallet custody happens to connect with other nodes to carry out its operation, to send and receive money effectively.

On the other hand, the bootstrap mode acts in the same way as the simple one, but the distinction is centered on the local node that will be able to store the Monero blockchain on the PC, this is one of the most secure options, but it demands a space of 120 GB of hard disk.

On the other hand, the advanced mode is to install the complete node, plus other additional functions, so it may be better to choose this one and create the new wallet, in the process you must save and take care of the seed phrase data, it is better to store it physically because digital can be stolen.

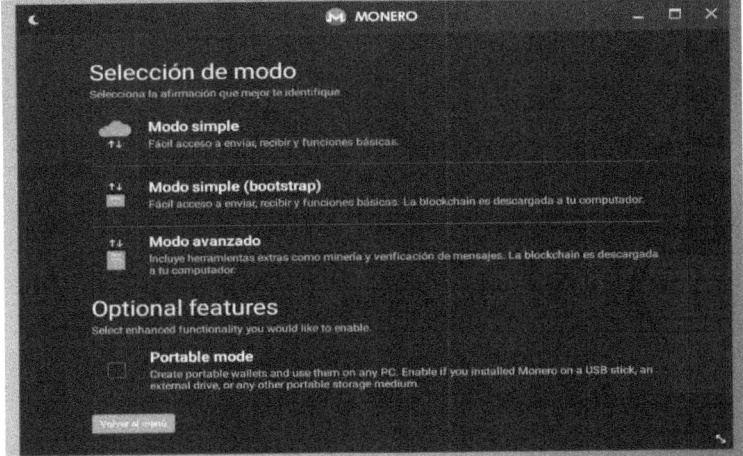

The next thing to do is to create a key for the wallet, it is best that it is robust so that any hacking attempt is complicated and with few possibilities, the rest is to finish the installation to have the wallet monero actively, this process takes place in the background without any problem.

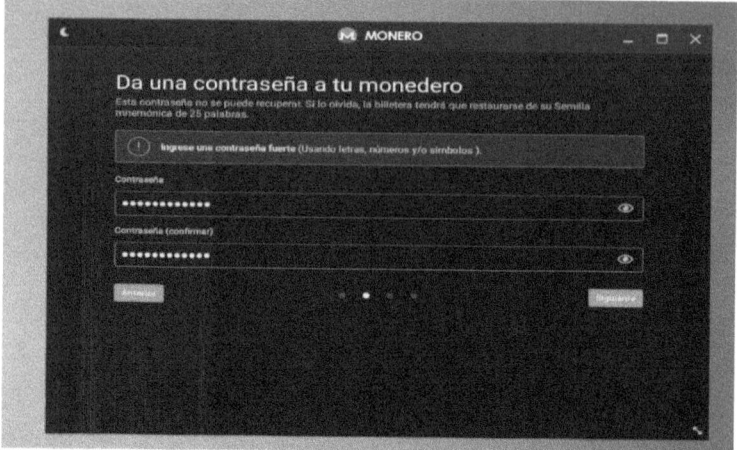

3. **Download the mining software to be used**

Downloading the mining software is the means through which this activity can be performed, the most common is to install XMR-Rig, thanks to its open source code that allows the download not to generate any adverse consequences.

4. **Choose the mining pool**

The best pool for mining is the one that is safe and close to your country, because in that way the performance of the mining power is similar, to find the best options you can enter www.moneropools.com, likewise another globalized alternative is www.supportxmr.com, since it has pools in several countries.

5. Adjusts the mining software

To start mining in Monero you must configure the program, for this you can use a website to make it a simple step, just look for the Wizard configuration, this is a function of XMRig where you can select "New configuration", to continue in; "add pool" or to choose another pool you must click on select Custom.

When choosing Custom because the pool does not appear in the menu, you can enter the necessary data provided by the pool, in case of selecting SupportXRM you can fill in the data regarding the wallet information in addition to the name of the worker, the next thing is to click on the mining method to be used.

In this way you can count on the configuration to use the pool you have selected, it is always advisable to request all the data so that it is not an interrupted process.

6. Configuring Monero

The most effective way to configure XMRig to start its operation is through the config.json file that is designed for this purpose, so you can open the file using a text editor or a notepad to delete the content and copy the one provided by XMR Wizard.

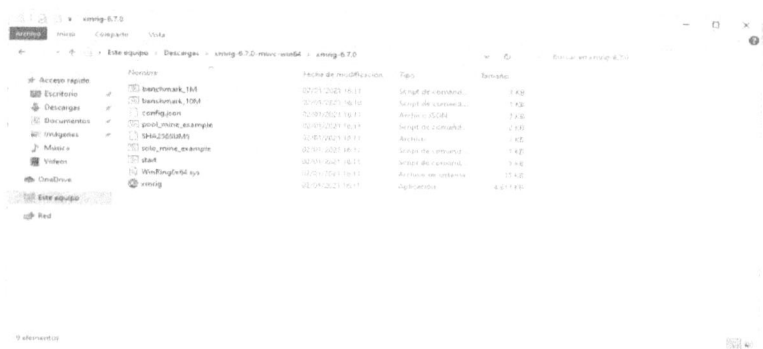

Once this step can be completed, the next step is to double-click on the xmrig executable so that you can start mining.

7. Applies mining equipment optimization

In case you are an advanced user, you can dedicate yourself to optimize the equipment and the mining program, this is possible through the command line to modify some options that have not been preconfigured, then depending on the power of the equipment you will begin to notice in a short time good results in the generation of income.

This means that Monero mining is simple and in a few steps, compared to other cryptocurrencies, so it is even possible to allocate equipment for mining in different pools that are part of this cryptocurrency with presence in several countries, but from the beginning you should know that mining alone is not a great option.

By mining through another methodology you can avoid the competition that exists in this area, especially because your earnings will depend directly on the hashrate that is part of the network, so joining a pool may be the best option, so you can take advantage of the striking movements of Monero.

Find out how to mine Zcash

Since the birth of Zcash in 2013 as a solution to the privacy of operations that Bitcoin does not offer, it has become an important focus within the field of mining, which is developed on the algorithm called Equihash, this is not compatible with the common type of mining hardware such as ASIC.

The mining development is much more correct by GPU, to be part of the block time of 1.25 minutes, to generate a reward of 6.25 ZEC tokens for each solved block, if this motivates you to carry out Zcash mining, you should start by investing in the necessary hardware and software to make a profit.

- **Hardware for Zcash mining**

It is necessary to have a mining hardware to run the software smoothly, but for this you must analyze the difference in performance on the GPU, CPU and ASIC, because they are types of computational power that matter when mining, this causes that each of these must be specified:

1. Mining with CPU

When mining an asset such as Zcash it is necessary to implement CPU processor power, for this reason it is most advisable to have a high performance which can be provided by AMD Ryzen Threadripper 1950x, plus 16 cores with a 32-thread processor, which would be estimated at about $900.

This way demands to take into account that when mining Zcash by means of CPU, it may be at a disadvantage compared to GPU, because the use of CPU has a low return on investment, so it is best to opt for GPU to achieve the expected gains.

2. GPU mining

The GPU mining medium employs pre-existing graphics cards on cryptocurrencies, which are ASIC resistant, this generates that you can more safely choose the GPU, as it is above the ASIC and CPU, to choose the most appropriate one you can consider AMD cards or those that are NVIDIA.

As the miner is based on the Equihash algorithm in this case, it can outperform MD cards, this requires that you must select a GPU card that has 1 GB of RAM, the most frequent options on the market is GTX 1080 for its energy efficiency, in addition to the GTX 1080 Ti which is powerful but expensive.

Other card options include the AMD Vega 56/64, which delivers good performance but with a high value, it is important to compare each quality with the price, to bet on the best performance.

3. **Mining with ASICs**

It had been previously reiterated that the Equihash algorithm presents resistance to ASIC hardwares, but Bitmain issued a statement about launching an ASIC for this type of miner that is compatible with Zcash, it is dubbed as Antminer Z11, surpassing the power of Z9 mini up to three times over performance.

The Antminer Z11 employment offers a hash power of 135 KSol/s, with a 12nm chip to demand a power consumption of 1418W under an energy efficiency of 10.50 J/Ksol, similarly another ASIC that can be compatible is Innosilicon A9 Zmaster, although it does not possess the same support.

- ## Zcash mining software

Once you have the hardware required for mining, the next step is to complete the installation of the Zcash mining software, for this you can find a good variety of software that are compatible to work with these software such as Zcash Mining Software, but it is a modality that works only with CPU.

What you can use or opt for is AMD GPUs such as Optiminer, Claymore and Genesis SGminer, as well as Nvidia GPUs within their options such as EWBF Cuda, Nicehash EQM, and NEHQ.

- ## Mine Zcash on your own or in a pool

Zcash mining alone at one time was profitable, but then the network hash rate became very high, to the point of needing a higher level of electricity and hardware, which in sum means that it is an expensive option, so the best alternative is to think with a mining group.

It is possible to choose solo mining, but with the premise that you can get a lower amount of ZEC gain, in addition to needing a high amount of GPUs, along with a higher level of electricity and willpower, it is better to opt for a pool that consists of grouping with other miners to increase the chances of earning tokens.

In a mining pool, each one of the miners unites their power, so that the puzzles of a blockchain can be solved more quickly, so that the profits are then distributed among the miners, distinguishing the computing power of each one, you can consult some pools such as Antpool, Coinotron, Coinmine, F2pool, Poolin, Zhash and others.

- **Zcash mining quote**

By means of a Zcash mining calculator offered by Coinwarz, you can evaluate the profitability of mining, especially taking into account the type of hardware you are using, since based on the hashrate it determines how much you can mine, without overlooking the energy costs and other rights of the miners in the case of a pool.

But it is a type of mining that is classified as simple, and the profitability varies depending on the timing of the cryptocurrency, so it is best to follow the estimates of Zcash mining profitability calculators, because it yields more current figure or data on prices, block times and hashrate.

To measure this type of activity, you only need to add the hardware type or model, plus the hash information, along with the profitability, to arrive at these results you can use calculators from CryptoCompare, WhatToMine, Coinwarz, and MyCryptBuddy.

Mining vs. investment; considerations at the outset

Learning and getting involved with mining requires time and perseverance to be a full-fledged part of this activity, so it becomes a highly lucrative choice, especially if you choose between mining on your own or through a company to do it in the cloud.

In case of being on your own, as mentioned above, you must have logistics and a large investment in hardware, especially those that are special for this type of purpose, so most people choose to do it through the cloud because it is more economical.

Examining and studying both options causes you to opt for the best path, especially because each has its benefits as well as its cons, this causes a thorough analysis is needed to identify the path that suits you best, from the beginning by

Bitcoin in 2009, the mining process emerged as a simple activity.

This means that previously with a personal laptop, which was not even fast, it was possible to generate profits over the world of cryptocurrencies, but then it raised its complication, although it does not mean that it is impossible to enter this kind of dynamics, it just means that it has been an industry that has evolved.

For this reason, Bitcoin can be mined in two ways, and if you know them well, you can take the risk and start looking for the profits you expect, considering the hardware prices and the difficulty of the mining activity, which has become hard work to make it a more meaningful investment.

However, the market also exerts its influence due to the volatile level, which is a broad challenge in order not to lose sight of the profits of this class of shares, for this you must follow the Bitcoin technology that currently makes few changes and its valuation does not plummet drastically.

It is vital to consider the following steps or scales before mining:

1. **Select mining company**

Cloud mining is exercised through the practice of renting mining hardware, so it is left to the other person to perform the work for the owner of the equipment or power, this kind of investment of equipment is paid in Bitcoin, regardless of whether it is not used to mine this specific cryptocurrency.

Before choosing this kind of alternative, it is best to thoroughly investigate the opinions of all those who use this way to generate income, especially because many companies decide to participate in this option, but then disappear, so it is best to opt for reliable companies that are respected to start with peace of mind.

There is a great diversity of options of companies to perform cloud mining, through CryptoCompare you can find a well assembled list with reviews to know the ratings of users, but it is vital to distinguish from options and proposals that only seek to postulate a scam.

2. Choose the mining package

Having the selection of the cloud mining company ready, with a formalized registration, the next thing is to prefer a mining package, where you choose by the amount of power, in addition to what you can get to pay, are the established agreements of what each party will do.

Normally by paying more commission, you can have access to a high level of performance, or a fast performance, but this is not a mandatory rule, to decide you can compare the offer of different mining companies, as you can also follow the actual value that is offered in the market.

Other aspects that also help to measure the most profitable side is the difficulty of mining that is set for bitcoins, in addition to the references that exist on the power that you are achieving through rent, but all these numbers change, they do not have a fixed offer far from it.

What you can do is to estimate how far a cryptocurrency like Bitcoin can take you to take that step, for all this you can use the Coinbase profitability calculator, where you can select some alternatives or variables to make a calculation to reduce your doubts.

These companies usually offer a contract fixed as a kind of pre-sale, this means that you must pay in advance, then when the hardware is available you can participate, this is not recommended because of the great risk of being scammed, in the end it is impossible to be 100% sure that it will be a profitable contract.

3. **Go to a mining group**

Once the contract has been established, the next thing to do is to join the mining pool, this means that this is the global mining team that you can join, this kind of alternative raises the chances of earning bitcoin through mining, and is defined as a standard practice.

Behind each mining pool there are also some pros and cons, you can take into account the type of low rates you can find, to classify this as the best opportunity, in this sense the most popular pool is Slush Pool, but it is also advisable to carry out a previous research because not all of them are reliable.

4. **Choose a wallet**

Completing the choice of the mining group, only leaves one last step such as having an account through which you will receive the bitcoins, because it is best that the cryptocurrencies are removed from the cloud, so that they can be managed from your wallet as a more secure modality.

Similarly, some companies offer the option of reinvesting your earnings, especially for you to use a higher dispersion power, the essential thing is that you think about what you will do with the bitcoins that you get from the mining work, since they are funds that you can even use in any store because of the acceptance they have.

Another measure you can opt for is HODling as a conservation of bitcoins, being a viable strategy to take advantage of some profitable moment of the asset, i.e. when the value of the asset grows, it will be favorable for the one who is storing this type of cryptocurrency to have a higher percentage.

It is not about being a financial advisor, but about following the predictions that emerge about cryptocurrencies, to make the decision about holding this asset class, even if you have hardware to deposit virtual currencies.

- **Mining bitcoins with your own hardware**

Before making any investment for mining hardware, you can use or apply a bitcoin mining calculator, so you can study each of the costs, because it is impossible to look at a profit rate without considering the costs that this kind of activity will generate.

Another aspect to consider are the prices that fluctuate due to the electricity issue, this kind of variables are a point to evaluate, for this reason it can be a costly action for many, and at the same time the possibility of obtaining profits can be low for a great amount of miners.

The configuration of the mining system is expensive, so what you should consider is the type of access you have to electricity, but under a cheap mode, the same applies to the internet connection, this must be a powerful resource, in turn this applies to the hardwares of ASIC miners that can be of the latest generation.

The hope of obtaining income through mining, demands the use of AsicMinerValue, you can observe all the technical requirements that this has, an ideal service for mining is through NiceHash where you can implement your own method, where each user can connect ASIC or GPU/CPU machines to rent them for mining.

The profits generated by mining, can be reviewed through the profitability calculator, to further consider the use of resources and therefore the cost it represents, thus you continue to measure the potential of this activity, to continue to assume the realization of mining or invest much more.

Minimum hardwares to mine Zcash and Ethereum

The general requirements that are demanded about mining Zcash or Ethereum, go hand in hand with the graphics cards that you can select, usually the favorites are AMD or graphics like NVIDIA, that way with either of these two hardwares, you can follow other compatible measures.

Cryptocurrency mining requires mostly a mining rig, by means of a whole series of minimum components to be able to use and take advantage of these systems, in every instant the consideration of the graphical aspect cannot be set aside, because it is a quality that deserves attention to visualize the profitability.

1. **Base plate**

In the midst of cryptocurrency mining you should not lack attention on the motherboard, as it is a key element and its selection represents everything, for that you can think of one that suits your needs, but for that you must know in advance the amount of graphics cards that will be installed.

Based on the number of graphics cards to be installed, because a model such as the Biostar TB 250-BTC is designed for six graphics cards, it costs 90 euros, while another option such as the Biostar TB250-BTC PRO works for up to twolvo graphics cards for 200 euros.

The important thing is that you can find a wide range of options in the market, but the common design is that they are for Intel processors.

2. **Processor**

The decision of the processor is very simple, because it is not necessary a very advanced type of processor, but a basic Intel Core i3 will be more than enough, in this sense they represent one of the most recurrent options, especially the Core i3 that are basic, by means of an accessible rate.

What happens with the processor is that during mining they do not support too much load, but everything is supported by the graphics card, in this sense the AMD are not considered because it is not usual to apply motherboards for this mode, so they are processors that are not supported as the main recommendation.

3. **RAM memory**

The variety of options on the RAM memory makes it an open decision, but the most basic is that it is from 4 GB of RAM, this is functional so that the program can run without problems, you can also opt for a module or two, it is best to make sure and use two modules to implement the Dual Channel configuration.

These memories must have heatsink to develop better performance, likewise when you want to sell them in the future, you will have more chances to do so, some prefer to raise the stakes and invest in a DDR4 RAM to carry out this action.

4. **Storage**

The hard disk drive can work without problems by means of an SSD, although an alternative as SATA that is SSD 120 GB works for this kind of activity, another possibility is to use some hard disk drive that is mechanical of at least 500 GB or 1 TB, that way you can leave without problems.

5. **Power supply**

The power supply requirement may be one of the most expensive points, but you can start from the minimum quality of 1000W, but based on the number of graphics cards you may need two power supplies, so you can extend the support on each of them.

The most valued is to bet on some model that offers 1250, so that it can support each graphics card, that is why it represents one of the heaviest investments, but it is a necessary component.

6. Graphics card

A key for mining is the function of the graphics card, in case of Ethereum for example, it is important to have AMD and the RX 570/580, or any other with similar qualities, but those that are not compatible are the RX Vega, instead Zcash can be mined through the use of NVIDIA, which works for other assets.

For this reason the decision or selection of cryptocurrency is an important preliminary step, that way you can choose a graphics card that can be widely compatible, the most appropriate from NVIDIA are GTX 1060 and any other GTX, but the top level of this range is GTX 1080 Ti.

7. Riser

It is known as one of the most indispensable elements to complement the mining rig, but it must be of version 6 to be able to offer the expected performance, by means of features that are a great opportunity based on the protection they generate and the simplest thing is that they have a low value.

8. Chassis

There are many doubts about the choice of the chassis, but in this case it is not a piece that you are going to use, since they do not have support for the level of the graphics card, so it is not possible to have a chassis, but in the market you can find solutions to cover this aspect, they can even be custom made.

All these elements add up to an overall investment of approximately 3,000 euros, all depending on the equipment you previously own, plus the value of the cryptocurrency you choose, plus the consideration of opting for a large room with plenty of ventilation, and the vision to sell the rewards at the best time.

The best GPU for mining Ethereum

Since the launch of NVIDA RTX 3060, there have been different opinions about this type of part, mainly because it is always looking to make a safe investment, this is easy to determine through its hashrate and the cost they have, so you can form a complete classification.

Cryptocurrency mining involves a set of prior decisions, one of them being the selection of the GPU in the market, as well as overcoming some setbacks such as power outages or the costs of this kind of service, all at the same time impacting on the deterioration of the GPU.

The initial concept is that graphics cards work as a positive support for gaming, so it can meet the demands of mining, following that premise you can inquire about the best GPUs to perform mining based on the hashrate they provide.

But when evaluating these aspects we also struggle with the fact that no hashrate is fixed, since a whole set of factors are involved, the first thing that sets the trend is the type of algorithm used, to this is added the type of speed that has the clock of the graph as well as the software optimization.

This in turn helps to mentalize in advance with the type of hashrate you can achieve or expect, in case of selecting Ethereum, for example, you would use the Ethash algorithm which is one of the most applied, starting from this idea you can know the brands and GPU models that are most employed and the type of hashrate you can expect.

Additionally to compare these pieces, we study the watt consumption and the type of profit you can estimate for 24 hours, but the final profit still depends on the value or what you pay for electricity consumption, classified as follows:

- **Nvidia RTX 3090.** It has 110 MH/s, 300W and 8.95 generated every hour.
- **Nvidia Rade on VII.** It generates 93 MH/s, about 200W with 7.57 of profitability per hour.
- **Nvidia RTX 3080.** It develops 91.50 MH/s, through 230W to throw 7.44 per hour.
- **AMD RX 6900 XT.** It delivers 64 MH/s, in exchange for 150W and about 5.21 every hour.

Within this classification what predominates the most is the RTX 3090 to carry out Ethereum mining, due to the fact that under the use of the Ethast algorithm it reaches a rate of 110 MH/s, but in contrast to this it is a card that requires up to 300 watts, therefore the electrical cost can greatly affect the gains.

Currently the best GPU card from AMD is the Radeon VII, because it has a performance of over 4 years, and offers 93 MH/s hashrate, in exchange for a power consumption of 200 watts, which indicates that it is an alternative that becomes quite cost-effective when calculating each of these details.

Similarly the mining performance of the RTX 3060, is very inhibited or limited, because it only reaches up to 42 MH/s, so it is lower than the performance of the RTX 2080, and the same goes for the RTX 3070 that only reaches 58 MH/s, this kind of discernment between one and the other is key to buy the best.

What is most commented is that the RTX 3060 has completed its cycle within mining, because it does not have good performance on modern algorithms that are designed to mine Ethereum, the same happens with the RTX 3060 TI that develops a limited performance, because what it seeks is that the graphics card is attractive to the gamer world.

That kind of focus on gamers, causes that for miners it is not enough, it is a matter of user preference, that is why NVIDIA is being closely watched, and if it reduces the hashrate then the best way will be to prefer AMD, although the Radeon model may be expensive or complicated to get, it will be a foresight to take.

Current Bitcoin mining facilities

The current restrictions in China have caused a change in Bitcoin mining, which is causing miners to look at this activity again, so the participation in this kind of activity has increased, especially because China used to generate 65% of mining worldwide, due to the price of energy.

But the Chinese government has implemented measures, to curtail mining activity up to 90% over the country, this has been known as a rough campaign, which decreases Bitcoin mining action the last days or months, this has been studied by hashrate generated over the country.

In the midst of China this type of measure has been studied, which overshadowed that 90% of the mining capacity that was being developed, therefore the mining sector in the country was totally minimized, as a consequence of this the mining plan has begun to be distributed over other areas of the world.

Because of the repression in China it was necessary to appeal to a parallel participation or in another location, this at the same time decreases the difficulty and turns it into a much more lucrative exercise, because it will no longer be an activity in demand, but it becomes easier and in turn profitable.

The reason why measures against mining have arisen is due to the environmental impact of this action, but in the same way this fact is defended in comparison to the degradation caused by minerals or precious metals, but in this case it is about the validation of transactions that are carried out between them.

The complexity of the operations has decreased, which in turn can lower the type of equipment needed to reach the solution of the mathematical puzzle, that mining process is what triggers rewards, being the main incentive to perform this kind of activity.

The best software to practice Ethereum mining.

The mining exercised through graphics cards, being a modality that has become frequent in recent years, in the case of Ethereum it is feasible to opt for graphics cards that can respond to mining software that merit prior study to make the best decision on AMD.

In the case of using AMD or NVIDIA graphic cards, different softwares are used that can support these pieces, such as ETHMiner, which is one of the most used for mining at present, this is special for the optimization function it has, especially for the Ethash algorithm.

But in the case of other algorithms may present failures by not supporting its operation, but you must remember that Ethereum mining lets you perform this activity on Ethereum Classic, Musicoin and others, at the same time the advantage of this software is its compatibility with Windows, Linux and MacOS operating systems.

It is vital to highlight that this type of software can work fully with AMD graphics, but it has been optimized by means of NVIDIA graphics, where the performance of solutions is concentrated on AMD GPUs, although they have a less desirable performance compared to other software.

- **GMiner**

It is a software developed by a set of Russian miners, which over time acquire a higher level of preference, initially developed by Equihash, but currently fails to support the operation of algorithms such as Ethash, ProgPoW and Kawpow.

That kind of algorithms have been added in 2020, where it offers support for Cuckatoo, Cuckaroo, Beamhash, Cortes and others, this software is available for operating systems such as Linux and Windows, without generating any problems with AMD and NVIDIA graphics cards.

The popularity of the software lies in the flexibility of the type of algorithms it is able to support, as well as the level of performance it offers, so it is a point of comparison not to be overlooked.

- **Best software with AMD and NVIDIA graphics combined**

One of the most curious options or applications within the world of mining, is the creation or formation of a mining rig for Ethereum but under the integration of AMD and NVIDIA graphics cards so that they can operate in turn, where the following alternatives stand out:

1. Claymora Dual Miner

This kind of software is designed for the Ethash algorithm, based directly on OpenCL, being a point that directly favors AMD, because it has kernels as assemblers so that they can be optimized, because it is a software that offers a lower amount of invalid actions.

The elements that are part of this software are not available elsewhere, they are special because once a failure is detected, the graphics card itself restarts as an automated response, this quality is striking because it means that you can combine an AMD and NVIDIA card on the same mining rig, with support for Linux and Windows.

• Ethereum mining software with AMD graphics cards

The most optimized within mining, is the use of AMD graphics cards, because it has great effectiveness on Ethereum, the most prominent that are frequently used are the following:

1. TeamRedMiner

A kind of software that has been developed to work uniquely with AMD cards, for that reason it can run a special optimization and is one of the pioneers in having the "zombie" option, this is an advantage for using graphics cards that are 4GB of VRAM.

In this case the size of the DAG reaches a higher size, but performance is lost when performing this kind of action, the support of this software extends to algorithms such as Ethash, Kawpow, Octopus, ProgPoW and also on Cryptonight, or other options, because it is an open alternative to these possibilities.

At the same time it is possible to carry out mining of other cryptocurrencies, with support and operation on Windows and Linux, so the download can be done from official websites, thus completing the list of the most used software for Ethereum mining, as well as for other cryptocurrencies.

Nowadays it is better to be specialized with the use of hardware and software, always hand in hand with the type of cryptocurrency chosen, because the solutions must be specific to what you are looking for or need, the essential thing is that they can be adapted to the needs and demands of this activity.

In case you want to continue using AMD graphics cards that are 4GB of VRAM, it can become interesting on this mining activity, this always plays or have direct relation with the logarithm used, there is a great variety of logarithms to choose from, the important thing is to get good performance.

www.ingramcontent.com/pod-product-compliance
Lightning Source LLC
Chambersburg PA
CBHW070120230526
45472CB00004B/1343